P U R E

Peter, thank you for coming to Catshill all those times,

P U R E

C A R O L

F R O S T

Carol Frost

TRIQUARTERLY BOOKS
NORTHWESTERN UNIVERSITY PRESS

E V A N S T O N

I L L I N O I S

TriQuarterly Books
Northwestern University Press
Evanston, Illinois 60208-4210

ISBN CLOTH 0-8101-5029-8
ISBN PAPER 0-8101-5004-2

Library of Congress Cataloging-in-Publication Data

Frost, Carol, 1948–
    Pure / Carol Frost.
        p. cm.
    "TriQuarterly books."
    ISBN 0-8101-5029-8 (cloth : alk. paper). — ISBN 0-8101-5004-2
(paper : alk. paper)
    I. Title.
PS3556.R596P87   1994
811'.54—dc20   93-43889
                                                            CIP

The paper used in this publication
meets the minimum requirements of the
American National Standard for Information Sciences
—Permanence of Paper for Printed Library Materials,
ANSI Z39.48-1984.

For

Harry and Dorothy

and for Win

for there is no place that doesn't see you

—Rilke

Contents

III

Acknowledgments

Some of these poems have appeared previously in the following publications:

The American Poetry Review: "Apple Rind," "Small," "Art," "Horror," "Recompense," and "Obedience"
The Atlantic: "Thrill"
The Gettysburg Review: "Country"
The Georgia Review: "Alto"
Ironwood: "Sunfish" and "Redbirds"
The Massachusetts Review: "The Argument"
The Missouri Review: "The Undressing" and "To Kill a Deer"
The New England Review: "Away," "Desire," "Nothing," and "Shame"
The New Virginia Review: "Refusal"
North American Review: "Mind"
Partisan Review: "Laws"
Pivot: "Her Beauty" and "Decoy Garden"
Ploughshares: "C.O."
Prairie Schooner: "Apple Rind," "The Snake Skins," and "Music"
TriQuarterly: "Pure," "Harm," "Apology," "Fury," "Truth," "Judgment," and "Crying Wolf"
The Virginia Quarterly Review: "Sexual Jealousy," "Balance," and "Fate"

"Sunfish" and "Apple Rind" appeared in *Chimera* (Peregrine Smith Books, 1990).

"Apple Rind" also appeared in *The 1992/93 Pushcart Prize XVII: Best of the Small Presses* (Pushcart Press, 1992). "Papilio" appeared in *The Bread Loaf Anthology of Nature Poetry* (University Press of New England, 1993).

The author wishes to thank the editors represented here and the National Endowment for the Arts for a fellowship in 1993 when I wrote the last poems for this book. I am grateful to many people who have been interested in these eleven-liners and who have offered encouragement, especially Margot Livesey, Richard Frost, and my friends at Bread Loaf Writers' Conference.

P U R E

Fate

Imagine: in the twilight of a river, trout rising to the hairs
        and netted wings
of water walkers, and yourself casting a baited line
toward shadows. There is no talking, and the mind learns
to drift, to take in the slightest signs, as if there's already
        begun
under the surface what will come to pass; it lures you
        along.
Reed, ripple, raccoon-scratches on the mud bank
lend their wisdom and their indifference to the moments
        before the pole bends double
or you give up, walk to the lighted house, and join the
        others at a table
to talk of life, love, logic and the senses, memory,
        promise, betrayal, character
and fate—the driving notion
that around the river bend a magnificent fish waits,
        prickling the black water.

I

To Kill a Deer

Into the changes of autumn brush
the doe walked, and the hide, head and ears
were the tinsel browns. They made her.
I could not see her. She reappeared, stuffed with apples,
and I shot her. Into the pines she ran,
and I ran after. I might have lost her,
seeing no sign of blood or scuffle,
but felt myself part of the woods,
a woman with a doe's ears, and heard her
dying, counted her last breaths like a song
of dying, and found her dying.
I shot her again because her lungs rattled like castanets,
then poked her with the gun barrel
because her eyes were dusty and unreal.
I opened her belly and pushed the insides
like rotted fruit into a rabbit hole,
skinned her, broke her leg joints under my knee,
took the meat, smelled the half-digested smell
that was herself. Ah, I closed her eyes.
I left her refolded in some briars
with the last sun on her head
like a benediction, head tilted on its axis

of neck and barren bone; head bent
wordless over a death, though I heard
the night wind blowing through her fur,
heard riot in the emptied head.

C.O.

For my son I tried to distinguish
   between personal fear and principle. Now laughter
      phlegms
deep in my throat because I remember the tenuous mud
      dam
   in the marsh, only surface tension holding
back the black water, and the sleek beaver
   gliding with a mouthful of sedge and sapling
back to the lodge and her yearling kits—the small
      miscalculation
   of her wake, and the dam's breach.
Like her I brimmed with solicitude,
   and now I can think of little else
but the beauty and the pleasure and principle
   of the world falling to watery bits.
There's nothing but danger, I wish I'd told him
   years ago. It betters you, forces you; sitting
in the sallows and the bath-warm water; raw, gray,
   asking more than you can bear.

Sweet, and unadulterated, my son cannot define like
      Aquinas

and Augustine the criteria for a just war,
circumscribing the mind, tightening the water's seams:
What does he have to do with death,
which insinuates, then drowns trees
near where the native orchids have begun to wilt
and where the beavers submerge, hidden?

Sunfish

Vertebrate, kin to the fully armed form
sprung upon the earth like Athena
from the head of Zeus, how is it no love

or scruples are stirred as you flap
at the end of my line, foul-hooked,
glistening? I recapitulate your gill slits

yet can't make of the life history of fish
a lesson, someone's first flounder
resurrected from a shallow grave,

water sparkling with green points of reflection
like tiny mirrors when green fry
swim out of their scales in fright.

There are no inhibitions, moments of hesitation,
no book of pain borne in your mind
when crawfish with lines tied to them

appear in the pond, and your muscleless face
is a mask the angler cannot pity.
I have held you—spinous, slimy,

and fragrant as dead leaves—in my bare hands
to admire your aegis of blue-green
and yellows shading into one another

as if formed by sunbeams through a shower,
and moments later pulled out your air bladder
with the hook. So naturally was death wrought,

I felt no evil, and so glorious the colors
lying on the surface of the water
robbed of moral.

The Undressing

They took off their clothes 1000 nights
and felt the plaster of the moon
sift over them, and the ground roll
them in its dream. Little did they know
the light and clay and their own sweat
became a skin they couldn't wash away.
Each night bonded to the next,
and they grew stiffer. They noticed this
in sunlight—there were calluses,
round tough moons on their extremities,
shadows under their eyes,
and sometimes a sour smell
they hadn't had as children.
It worried them, but at night the animal
in their bodies overcame their reluctance
to be naked with each other,
and the mineral moon did its work.
At last when they woke up and were dead,
statues on their backs in the park,
they opened their mouths
and crawled out, pitifully soft and small,
not yet souls.

Fury

And the whole night she had told herself to be pleasant
as she lay by the sleeping man, and she'd gladly have
        listened to herself,
but as the enormous dawn sneaked into their darkness
and seized them in its paws, she found herself with the
        old fury,
past her carefullest politeness. She saw she'd need
        millennia to find a way
to comprehend the reason for the difference between
        their early ideals—
a garden where plums and peaches grew well and tasted
        wild
and they were unembarrassed by genitals—and what had
        become of them.
This apple-pose. It was no good blaming God or Adam,
        she knew, but she couldn't help herself—:
Why hadn't the one spoken forthrightly and had the
        other caved in?
Then, hardly allowing him to fully awaken, she said her
        first sarcasm. Then another.

Apple Rind

Someone else was afraid and spoke to me
and I couldn't answer . . . swallowing oxygen
from a tube. And then? The cool blade
freeing rind from an apple
like the first touch of day. How long
I'd been in someone's still life—the blade
hidden, dividing—and was helpless.

Perfectly drugged, I lay just shy of winter
in my own mind. My cut chest felt nothing,
no terror, no pain. And there were morphine's sweet-
and-fruit boxes piled on the white terrain
like reasons for lives and death.
The orchard was weathered to admonitory bareness
except for a few frozen apples
above a disturbance of snow—the hoofprints
of deer coming by several routes to this late harvest,
the dim haunches and various limbs
afloat on movement that can break
or double back into the gray calm of woods.

How to explain directions a mind takes
or why I told no one how much I wanted
to come back to this beautiful, stupid world.

Pure

He saw that the white-tailed deer he shot was his son;
it filled his eyes, his chest, his head, and horribly it
     bent on him.
The rest of the hunting party found him hunkered down
     in the grass,
spattered like a butcher, holding the body as it kept
     growing colder in his arms.
They grasped his elbows, urging him to stand, but he
     couldn't. He screamed then
for Mary and Jesus, who came and were present. Unable
     to bear
his babbling, and that he might no longer have to be
     reproached, the men went to get help.
He only had left to him his pure hunter's sense, still clean
     under his skin,
a gun, the example of wounds, a shell's ease in the
     chamber, as he loaded,
the speed of the night chill, while his mind like a saint's
     tried to bear
that which God took from His own mind when he could
     not, not for another moment. . . .

II

Sexual Jealousy

The queen mole, who is unequivocal,
exudes a scent to keep the other females neuter
and brings forth the colony's only babies, hairless and
      pink in the dark
of her tunneled chamber. She may chew a pale
      something, a root,
find it tasteless, drop it for the dreary others to take away,
      then demand
more; she must suckle the young. Of course
they all hate her and are jealous of the attention given her
by her six bedmates. In their mutual dream she is dead
      and her urine
no longer arrests their maturing. As irises infallibly
      unfold,
one of their own will feel her sex grow quickest and
      greatest. As they dig
together, their snouts full of soil, they hope this and are
      ruthless in their waiting.

Truth

Those who can neither cast out of their hearts false
        feelings
nor look beneath the riding images
on a river, for a second life—all the details of scraping
        fin—are harried
by the one who gropes, to no end
save sight, for the beginnings of beauty or truth. Ugh.
The sorority girl has social obligations. The political
        science majors
have politics on their minds. Must they sit over a plot's
        depth
and try to see its secret and raise it dripping, thick, into
        the classroom? What if
it quivers and still smells like the river bottom, the sky's
        leavings?
Someone cracks a joke and they all laugh like inquisitors,
like revolutionaries swept along the surface of an
        immense current.

Thrill

To say fabricated things, where freedom is forced
on young girls,
and give it your own sensual twist, pretending in their
 bodies'
natural curves lies a willingness like animals to lick and
 rub each other
in the soft afternoon light. To thrill yourself with the
 imagined scent
of bodies redolent with oil and mango-colored.
And if a child's face releases a shadow,
no longer able to quiet herself with herself (*what*, for you,
 is wrong?),
to force her on to an ever deeper bliss—a nude queen
 lying on a green carpet,
a servant picking yellow fruit, and two old men near a
 large tree
discussing The Tree of Knowledge, your favorite scene.

Horror

When horror, that with pretty masks
no longer stood to one side as he walked from his house
      to the garden,
extolling neither the magic of the atmosphere nor medals
      that he had earned for painting,
but indefinable, still deferred—
as if somewhere a prophet had put down his hood and
      bellowed—,
grew colossal, Goya put fourteen versions of it on his
      interior walls,
the most audacious a dog whose trespasses have sunk him
      in an abstract grave.
That he cannot go to the Master toward whom he is
      looking is in the slight blue stain
in the dog's eyes; that Goya wanted the whole room to
      see how terribly the dog wanted
to go is in the tipped yellow absence above his head. This
      is how it was and how it is: caught,
wholly tempted, without a clue. How little has art driven
      off.

Judgment

The angel that rebellion raised was never able, right up to
    the end,
to leave Him alone or help solidify, by saying either "yes"
    or "no," His cloudy sense of things,
but kept intruding, even in His dreams, with doubts and
    questions.
It was a nightmare inhabited by dolls
and dead persons, winged souls, wretched lambs and
    lions that grew in Him
and made Him waffle, and twisted with self-hate. In His
    mind it was the angel who pushed
until He pushed back, then the angel flew off like a mad
    man
to earth and buried himself with the lowest
creatures, as reproach; and in His mind the beauty
of this arrangement suddenly shone in a fire's glare of His
    own powers to make judgments
that no longer hurt Him, and so He gave it names.

Laws

She knows of doom only what all women know,
deciding not to speak of it, since speech pretends
its course can be made to bend:—someone fleeing hot
    and sweating
and the victors close behind, then two roads all at once in
    a wood. Which one leads
farther away? Under cover of silence
she goes along as if nothing would happen to her,
swayed by breezes—dazed, her friends say in their
    concern,
after having called or dropped by.
Once, late in her illness, in the heat of a morning walk,
she raises her wig and shows us this surge of white back
    from the forehead. The tablets
Moses carried, with his guesses, in the end could not have
    been more blinding or more lawful.

Music

You are right. At death I might well desire both day and
        rest,
some calm place where light is stabilized on an arbor,
a table, green glasses, and damask. The taste is of earth
        and sunlight,
tomatoes with folds at the blossom end and a large rough
        navel
with a bit of stem still attached, oil with basil
and lots of garlic, causing thirst for wine. And the music
to be played at my funeral must be the sound of the
        rosined bow
working against the wind, not old keys that are only
        echoes, but strange
gold in the beetle's click, a jay, a three-color bird, a
        brown thrush,
their asides and intimations like the napkin songs
of great composers, written before the last bread and
        wine are gone.

Art

Why when she gave her memory a mother whose cruelty
    was godly,
and who was beautiful, and the North African boy of
    twenty
in the Paris of her youth, who tore down
his fresco at the end of every day because the cement
    hardened
before he could paint his red angels—*Je ne sais quand,*
    he'd say—
and memory *knew* she loved them, did it refuse to say so?
    She imagined she saw its gorge fall,
as after swallowing, and her own mouth felt like cotton.
She wanted to write it all down. What could tell her she
    would have to forget herself,
her art, everything, and make herself stare at a lake where
    a dragonfly stared
at a tree, at nothing, then deposited its eggs in the still
    water and left,
as if it trusted or could go on without?

Mind

As he went on—no one else in the yard, late, well past
        dinner—stacking cordwood,
it was as if his body, supple and allayed
by sweat, were surrendering to something larger than
        itself, unpossessed
by moonlight, so that when from the shadows, head-
first, exhausted, August fell, he sensed it; it was neither
        the wind,
nor the dark that so increased in all things they almost
        perished,
but more like a theater curtain drawn back—: There
        stepped
lives not completely lived,
yet inflamed, and a wooden staircase. Out of death and
        promises he'd made,
his mind, in rhythm with the lateness of the world,
that turning, saw absence and its presentiments step
        down, as if free.

Apology

Already the land is starting to forget gardens;
reminiscences no longer hold the heart completely
as someone held her a little roughly once in somber sweet
       groves,
and the touch she was utterly dissolute to, that caused
       collapse behind her knees,
sunslides in the lake, she feels a resistance toward,
       then apology,
as if a thorn catching her sweater has torn a small hole—
       as if she shouldn't
have worn the sweater. What induces
then weakens the greater and lesser passions is what she'd
       like to know.
—Something like the green underneath red and yellow
       which is now wilting
has left her body; and she is someone who *had* loved
and is no longer availing and can neither take nor give
       away.

Her Beauty

By now her beauty no longer catches glances like small
      animals in a gentle snare,
autumn having thinned the light and frozen its blossoms
      in the field.
Even her looks of imprecation and her frowns seem weak,
and she says fond, foolish things about herself,
about once having been greatly admired, envied, fated—
a Psyche to Venus—and how she loved her husband who
      was faceless
and gave her pleasure. Better than pretending
indifference—like the heaping snow;
better to say what she by another once had known,
only so secret and withdrawn the way it is in the
      mornings,
in weather, an animal's fur bristling, a moleskin.

Shame

Like one in reverie, so she stood, holding the clay pot on
      the table to her.
It was as if she'd laid her forehead that was again smooth
      on her lover's naked chest
and he held her until they no longer trembled. And there
      was no end.
In her late decade she still found within herself
the evening that waits till it be evening again.
Her smile was uninjured, quietly daring the others in the
      room—:
For everything her freckled hands did touched a familiar
      dark place
that vibrates—taking what was left of herself
and her long gone youth,
and all of her sex, together as a bow's stroke does.
O shameless song.

Desire

To be swayed by everything—:
the pelican whose wings fawn on the slightest breeze
and the yellow fish flowing into its empty, reeling brain
are like the desire that cannot be kissed away.
It breeds in the space thrown between them. You know:
the hope of even seeing you again is slipping from me,
but a scrim of images resists, hangs on the air,
even as I speak of other things to people who know
      you—
not weather, but the strong shoulder, your face burnt
      brown as cork.
At every effort, every try, I remember, coasts slid into
      yesterday.
Hell was certain.

Balance

is how you carry it, how it is; for example, the turkeys
    which seemed ordinary—grazing through
the piled brush for butternuts, all head and feathers, then
    taking the shot because they didn't see
you standing on a stump,
one dying outright, the other baffled, half rising in the
    brown light and batted
to the ground—how ungainly large they made the
    afternoon, heaping up out of slopes,
trees, torn pieces of clouds
an excitement. When you stopped running, you took
    them from under your jacket,
where they had kept shifting and threatening to slip out,
still with a bit of warmth in them, and grasped one in
    each hand
by its horned feet like handles to steady yourself, leaning
    into the
land's steepness and accord, growing used to them, their
    difference.

Crying Wolf

Not howling, but from within the deep wildness of all
      things, assailed on all sides
by the nightmare of nations, walking and flying specters,
      chimeras, nils,
which can't be outrun or waked, and which snows no
      longer bury,
came a sound as forlorn as when the heart devours the
      prophet. He lowered his head
at land's end after the wind took away the last of the
      sound and, in the silence,
the hair on the back of the neck of the world froze.

Nothing

She turned away. And her child slid toward
the ice edge of the precipice, gravity and momentum
      wrestling on his shoulders.
She could not bear to see the outcome and was starting
      to pretend he did not exist;
if his existence would come to an end. See: there is a
      snowy peak and clouds
spilling so softly they create a whirlpool of silence. She
      lets herself be in it.
She no longer hears anything. Not the wind. Not the
      scraping shoes. Not him.
How she used to fret, to brush the hair back from his
      eyes
so everyone could see his beauty and she could see the
      least shadow
of sorrow or illness. But there is nothing left to do for
      him.
Since the forces like acrobats keep somersaulting and
      playing
with him, she will not hearken or give them the pleasure
      of her scream.

Harm

She had only begun to get used to her body's exposures
to pain, like the insinuations behind questions: winter
asking the tree, where's your strength?— a priest asking a
    soul, where's your marrow?
Aversions, truth, invective,
it wasn't her answers which mattered, only her lying on a
    bed
being administered shocks until the world grew tired
of experimenting with another bit of clay and the inward
    liberties. So it seemed.
And when the intern came into the room, asking how she
    was
and snouting through her chest with drainage tubes, as
    strong a desire
as she'd ever had rose up in her. She must have gestured,
    or he already knew, because,
as if in expectation, he smiled at her and stepped out of
    harm's way, backward, for just a moment.

Recompense

That time, long practiced in pinning the alligator's jaw
       between his chin and chest,
the wrestler swam wearily, with long, blind hands and
       arms,
toward the brown eyeknobs, ignoring the crush and
       pester of the crowd
above the gator hole. And when the reptile bit,
he felt himself torn open, left exposed, accused—: fiercely,
that somehow a new existence could be formed out of
       the old. He remembers he rotated
with the alligator, attending to its muscularity,
pulling it down to the river bottom where its heart gave
       out and it drowned.
He tore the white belly skin for a belt. He took the
       stomach stones
as recompense for his disfigurement. —And all the while
       saving the crowd's glances,
which were tinged with respect, though some eyes wept
       and some looked at the darkening bayou.

Secrecy

It lay and dried in the sun, puffing, then losing its
    coherence,
and there was a sudden sickliness
in the air when the wind lifted and blew across to her, as
    if in ambush: cotton
and sweet chloroform. She ducked down and away,
    holding her breath, and went on
until she could sense no longer what wept and ran from
    the raft of skin.
It was as if someone had risen up, unwashed, bearded,
    from a copse,
and tried to come too near—with a gesture of
    supplication, knowing
that she was half-willing, tempted by strangeness
    (a bouquet
of lilacs in a beggar's hands)—and almost succeeded. But
    it grew
too intense, menacing. She shied. It was scarcely
    explainable
and could not be kept a secret. A branch lightened into
    place. Everywhere things decayed.

Small

Boa, once when you were small, you ate small things.
Now you clasp to yourself the fat peccary like a bride
to soften with caresses. Have you read the Scriptures?—
" . . . out of the eater came forth meat and out of the
       strong came forth sweetness . . ."—
I do not think this gorging can be right. Your brother
       who tried to swallow the moon
lost his arms; the knife cut asunder his joints. He was
       defiled, spat upon, burned
because of our detestation for overstepping oneself. Look
       at you settling in the dust for a nap,
pig-bellied, sweet stinking. Will you sleep six months?
       Will you wake fiercely hungry?
Beware. When it comes to people, you'll have to think of
       religion, Eden, ethics committees,
all that fuss. So eat two mammals next time, but the four-
       legged kind.
Never the pinkness and honey of the human.

Obedience

(the nuns)

Mostly they say normal things,
eating partridge and beans, drinking more water than
      wine,
and we save up our glances until they file out and two
      waiters come to clear away
plates and to put down a clean tablecloth. Before the
      waiters are done we take a picture,
illuminated by a wall lamp. Doesn't someone always sit
      among us
like this, grown stronger from an important death or an
      intolerance—in street clothes
or habit—yet overlooked, even discredited (a saint, but a
      headstrong saint)?
All ate, but one ate more austerely. All spoke, but it was
      her words which unsettled
her friends, the judgments of whom are obedient but can
      be swayed.
And so we have inflicted endless pain. Only bread crumbs
      and empty bottles
are left, as if they scattered the moment. We resolve so
      little.

Refusal

Because the acres were not smoothed with topsoil, she
wrenches
the handmower into places the rider won't reach. Afraid
of snakes. Hating the thistle.
A keening from blade hitting rock goes into her ear like
an insistent beak in alder,
and she stops, repulls the starter, and leans in hard again
to move the engine
through the undergrowth. Her tall boys, men really, and
their father have long since
ceased wanting to know why, sweating, thorn-tattooed,
she pushes the doubtful edges
of the yard back, cutting paths through a dead
predecessor's orchard:
not to name wildflowers or to watch the delicate
metamorphoses unfold and unfold
in green billowed darkness; not to smell mint. How to
describe the beauties of this
violence and this fatigue, even to herself? Isn't there a
human stillness in shapes labored
over, and comfort to be taken from feeling nature's
refusal to be much moved?

The Past

Was it in stepping into dusk? Did a glance release this
    turbulence
where Martin's fields thicken with thorn apple and a
    migratory bird makes
a sound?
Not even the quick flowering of April winds alters it,
    what a man in a straw hat
bending down
above the scythe's reach found, only now so saturated
    with rust and greatly indrawn,
the way it is in the past.
Yet the blade seems to will itself to hold an edge,
    expressing the kind of time
which plays around the roots of the grasses, and still
    knows, still passes,
still causes shadows
to seem to fit themselves around the ankles, refusing
    separation.

Music II

Yesterday two blackbirds splashed, like cymbals, into the
      lilac bush,
disappearing, or flying
and skimming the undulations of the hayfield beyond,
and the composer abstracted them. Only after many
      hearings of his concerto
may we comprehend the russet-blue of their initial
      noise
and—with help of notes and staff—realize their particular
      music:
What an imperious thirsting after the sun, as they lift,
and what melancholy, for a morning, when all this fire
and these clouds come together. There, beside us now,
      roams Pan—listen how
shadows tremble, massing in the canebrake and rue
      anemone as he plays,
as if their edges burned. Hear the can-bear-it-no-longer
      moment assume them.

Alto

The day of chorus when she was sent out
for singing wrong notes, for conceiving
herself a soprano, she stood in the hallway.
Behind the door voices braided Bartók
into garlands. She had never been so ashamed.
See the roses, blooming yonder,
far from dead leaves—she heard the words
and saw the soprano notes perched breathlessly
above the staff, the red and orange vapors
making melody. She'd sung with the tenors
when they had the melody.

                             But now
she told herself this would be her lesson.
Outside the chorus room, the bottom
of the music brought her back, the darker voices,
she thought, like shadows in the song.
And though she listened for the unisons
as if for the meaning of a garden of roses,
when she went back into the room, the air
was filled only with the stale essence of their breath.

III

Country

Tables, chairs, a used refrigerator in a thicket
Of zinnias; a woman lifting a window blind;
A man crippled with fat who waves hello,
His dog on a short chain prowling in front
Of his angry shed, the fur unkempt and bearding,
Fervent as Rasputin to wrench free
And get to a new voice and a stranger's scent,
The garden primeval
With snails, wrung with yesterday's rain;

And the tire gardens, the pink and yellow rubber
Ringing the geraniums; the established names on the
          mailboxes
And gravestones weathering the rich light;
And the smell of old lilacs; the tin advertisements
For farm machinery rusting on the milk houses;
The lines of light between planks
Crookedly spaced; wasps' nests; starlings';
The surveyor's orange flags; the wrecked autos
Like speciality stores in a fenced lot;

And the auction block, the brisk rhythm
Of selling—going, gone—it is a journey
They no longer can keep ahead of, as under a tent
A revivalist and congregation melt
Into one large droning; or it is a big top,
The women tidying the trailers, tidying the junk,
With *Lonesome Road* on the radio, the men drinking beer
Around the clock, revving their engines,
And the mutt at leash end crashing left and right.

The Snake Skins

The intrigue of this house
is a snake in the foundation, disturbed once
out of his stone place
by a laborer who was removing part of the floor

and southern wall, its lath and crumbling plaster,
to add a sliding glass door.
There were five or six shed skins,
like a multiplication

of the snake's slithering
so close beneath the whispers the night
provoked us to hear and our bare feet.
Now, though more variance of light

pours into the century-old house, flux
and equinox,
and though the laborer cut in half the snake,
I think in darkness, deep in the recesses

of air and dust, in edifices
thought solid, of the little motions

going on, breeding snakes that may
and may

not be meek. I only know
of the spotted adder dead long ago
and these skins like gloves for individual fingers.
I suspect there are others.

The Argument

Here is the cold, strict cell of the terrorist.
He is sorting through pieces of metal.
In front of him a pipe, wires, detonator, and a clock:
premises to follow through to the end.

If from an open bedroom door upstairs
a whimper or a sigh comes, he listens
until silence develops again, then turns
to the pile of shrapnel and pours it into the pipe.

Angels elbowing each other off the head of a pin
are not more violently correct,
nor more delicate, as he connects each part,
thinking, perhaps, of how the entrails and heart

are the House his declarations will be made in.
He has already scanned the newspaper for the date and
        time,
and he knows his victim's movements.
This is what I meant, what I meant

all along, you idiots, he says with his careful hands.
Why can't you understand
right and wrong aren't wired to the same clock?
Not today. Not now. Not my clock.

Then he sets the timer and lays the bomb in its cardboard
        tomb,
seals it, his saliva on the stamps,
and sends it to me, to you.
No chance to demur or turn leftist or wear a new swastika.
Not when he's finished and turned off the lamp.

Papilio

Collecting is a basic human trait. The great collectors
found the Nabokov Pug, *suvarovius* flying by the
  hundreds,
and the common glider, then spread their wings,
  medicating them
so carefully that no corruption invaded; they placed
them in beautifully carved bureaus to remember
the graceful madnesses of their flight over the white
  clearings,
the dark green ferns, the wildflowers, and the peculiar,
  crooked branches
of the thornapple like crucifixions. Some lay their eggs
  near violets;
some need the salts and minerals in animal urine;
most are diurnal. The only time I held one in my hand
was when I found it in my garden, fanning itself
on a bean plant. It seemed to have muscles in its wings,
but all I could see, on closer inspection, were its veins, its
  curled proboscis,
and its horrible compound eyes, like those on the fallen
  preening angels

of the imagination. I like to think that its letting me pick
   it up
was a sign of its complicated instinct for survival—in the
   way its eyespots
can persuade birds to peck at a dispensable part of its
   wings.
When I let it go, it wafted over to the barn wall.
What trick of pen or brush could capture that slightness
of flying? No wonder they are pinned to boards,
   romantics exaggerate
their delicacy, and modern poets dislike them. But they
   are not frail.
Think of their long thin hearts pumping yellow blood,
   their concealed poisons,
and their pheromones and colors which are sexual—they
   grow transparent
from sex. They are also territorial. Think of the rate of
   speed of autumn.

Redbirds

The redbirds gathered
in the pines railing the hill
behind the house, the snow grew

colder and empyreal,
and the moon moved into place
in the east. Then

the flock swayed
and was gone, the horizon
crowned by empty iodine.

There were animal tracks
knee-deep, dark troughs
of snow to follow,

and sounds of wind, night's feints
white and stinging
in the rack of winter boughs.

As long as I walked in the absence
of the redbirds, my eyes attuned
to such vague cages

of light as were, shadows took
the shape of Yeti
or winter lion,

frightening beyond sense,
but all the time going away.
I tried to look past

the dense dark,
beyond the close,
beyond whatever closes

when redbirds plunge off the crest
of a hill, but saw only
the chilly reaches of snow.

Who shall say
when I reach the crest of the hill,
the shadows will not be deep

and gray as now
and the world
not have an exit

but a farther field
waning west,
the winds off that snow

cold as fence wire, and no harp?

Decoy Garden

How the hum of the garden thins when I come near,
first the birds' plaited cries,
rustles in nearby undergrowth,
and the droning of bees at blossoms,
sucking sap; the country's greedy
life. It's a shambles,
the plot I packed with seeds left in the bottom
of their packets, as decoy;
yet even as the peas are torn and cropped,
it brims, like a trencher on the table of the highborn.

Although I've never gone hungry,
I hoard rice and cans of beans—
enough for several months without order across the land,
and for winter.
                 After the rains relent
I plant a double garden,
half where dew lies along the rows, like peace,
and the other to tempt out of their holes
and burrows the hungry clothed in fur.
I know they are in the shadows waiting to enter
at first light with their teeth and claws.

As I walk back to the house, the sounds return,
twitching beneath the air's soft vellum and palpable as
     flesh,
as if I were hearing and seeing the origin of appetite—
the belly swelling and the open mouth.

Away

Their breasts and abdomens filled with air,
   grayleg geese soar on thermals,
between god's feet and hair.

The autumn light is silver and rose, foreign,
   and their flight is like some distant,
almost invisible allegory of what has gone

out of a person's life,
   less like the dying away of a chord
than a handful of pomegranate seeds, and Perseph-

one. The bodies of geese are light,
   the bones porous, hollowed to extreme thinness,
built exactly right

for leaving the gravel bed, and I imagine
   their tender, lazy lack of heart
as the trees rage into another season.

II

Just as the spring, which somehow begins
   and is nowhere, changes, or a hand
which reaches for an unexpected reason

and doesn't take my hand, not yet,
   so the somewhere that lies beyond me
becomes a disfigured garden, cold and wet,

yet not all there. It's as if it longed for me,
   or not for me. I heard voices, tender, primal,
speak to me, sing to me,

and remain a sorrow. And the hot
   air one September slathered my back and shoulders
with wax so that the colored leaves caught

there like feathers. Lightly,
   as after death, I imagine myself in skies past this one,
for there's no one anyplace who isn't secretly

going away.

Winter without Snow

The man carried bucket after bucket of plaster dust
up the earthen ramp of the barn that caught fire
and emptied each as if he were dumping snow
onto the blackened beams.
In the trees there were little glass seeds,
souvenirs of winter without snow.

When the man turned back toward the house,
he wore a helmet of dusty mother-of-pearl
and his eyelashes were silvery half-moons.
I watched him with all the coldness I had
yet it would not snow.

Nothing could make it snow.
Not the burst water pipes, the leggings,
the sleds, or the white horses.
Not the smoky fountains, the clouds.
They were souvenirs of winter without snow,
as was my wish for a white field
like a fresh beginning.